Never the
Whole Story

Never the Whole Story

POEMS BY

Anita Skeen

MICHIGAN STATE UNIVERSITY PRESS ▪ *East Lansing*

⊚ The paper used in this publication meets the minimum requirements of ANSI/NISO
Z39.48-1992 (R 1997) (Permanence of Paper).

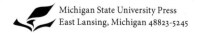 Michigan State University Press
East Lansing, Michigan 48823-5245

Printed and bound in the United States of America.

17 16 15 14 13 12 11   1 2 3 4 5 6 7 8 9 10

LIBRARY OF CONGRESS CATALOGING-IN-PUBLICATION DATA
Skeen, Anita.
Never the whole story : poems / by Anita Skeen.
p. cm.
ISBN 978-1-61186-003-0 (pbk. : alk. paper)
I. Title.
PS3569.K374N48 2011
811'.54—dc22
2010042320

Cover design by David Drummond, Salamander Hill Design
Cover artwork is "untitled #17" and is used by permission of the artist,
Guillermo Delgado.
Book design by Charlie Sharp, Sharp Des!gns, Lansing, Michigan

green
press
INITIATIVE   Michigan State University Press is a member of the Green Press Initiative
and is committed to developing and encouraging ecologically responsible
publishing practices. For more information about the Green Press Initiative and the use
of recycled paper in book publishing, please visit *www.greenpressinitiative.org.*

Visit Michigan State University Press on the World Wide Web at
www.msupress.msu.edu

For my parents,
John and Bea Skeen,
and my grandmother,
Flossie Pruden,
who taught me the old hymns,
who gave me the gift of story and song.

Acknowledgments

"Woman with Something to Say" was part of a poetry and art exhibit entitled *Woman With. . . .* at Ghost Ranch Conference Center in Abiquiu, New Mexico, in October 2003.

"Ghost House" and "House of the Rising Sun" were part of a poetry and art exhibit entitled *Furnishings* at Ghost Ranch Conference in Abiquiu, New Mexico, in October 2004.

"Remembering My Father, Struggling" and "But Not Forgiving Myself" were semi-finalists in the *Nimrod/ Hardman Pablo Neruda Prize Competition* in 2006 and were published in *Nimrod, Awards 28* in October 2006.

"Oklahoma Family Portrait, 1928," was previously published in *Cadence of Hooves,* edited by Susan Jantz. Yarroway Mountain Press. 2008.

"Vocabulary Night" was previously published in *Once Upon a Place: Writing from Ghost Ranch,* edited by Anita Skeen and Jane Taylor. Night Owl Books. 2008.

"Button Bag" and "What the Seed Knows" first appeared on the blog *The Secret Lives of Things* (http://livesofthings.wordpress.com/), posted by Guillermo Delgado and Anita Skeen, fall 2009.

"In the Garden" first appeared at http:/lansingonline. com/news/poemaday, April 23, 2010.

I would like to express my deep appreciation to the Virginia Center for the Creative Arts, where I was selected a Fellow in April and May of 2006, allowing me time and space to work on *Never the Whole Story*. I also thank the faculty and participants of the Ghost Ranch Creative Arts Festival and the Fall Writing Festival for providing me over the years the atmosphere and support that contributed to many of these poems. I'm eternally grateful to my long-time writer and reader friends Ina Hughs and Jane Taylor, Jeanine Hathaway and Carol Barrett, for their conversation about and encouragement of my work. Almost finally, thanks to Martha Bates, the best editor anyone could ever have, and certainly the most patient. Then, finally, to Beth Alexander, who for thirty years has been so much a part of the story.

Contents

LOVE LIFTED ME

LET THE LOWER LIGHTS BE BURNING

I Love to Tell the Story

I love to tell the story,
Because I know 'tis true;
It satisfies my longing
As nothing else can do.

—Catherine Hankey/William C. Fischer

Never the Whole Story

... *every detail is an omen and a cause.*

—Jorge Luis Borges

In Cottageville,
Kinsey Pruden carved
into the stone chimney;

a snowflake falling, hesitant, not knowing
whether to go it alone;

one shoe spilled on the shoulder
of I-75;

our kitchen table, model car parts
strewn across newspapers, instructions
a wad on the floor;

the window open, screen torn;

a tea bag dropped in the Styrofoam cup, kettle
chitchatting on the stove;

at noon, my mother in her recliner,
one cat in her lap, the other draped like a doily

on the chair back,
sleeping;

Coleman lantern, swinging down the trail;

grizzly on the slope,
tourists pointing, above;

the bed never slept in,
drawers empty,
door unlocked;

a notebook open on the table, sentence
unfinished;

your hand with the ring, your hand without;

the old home place collapsing, blue
Mason jar in the grass,
faceted with light, my birthstone.

Letter to an Unknown, and Probably Deceased, Photographer

It must have been seventy years ago
you took that shot, my grandmother standing
in front of the front of a car, whitewall tire
practically up to her waist, running board
streamlining the side. A log house
backgrounds the car, square
logs, good chinking, grounded
and going nowhere. My grandmother
wears a dress dotted as the Milky Way,
a Sunday dress, and a wide straw hat
circles her head like the rings of Saturn.
She is looking at you with a difficult
smile, this woman who by now
has had a husband drown
and three daughters arrive, all
before her twenty-fifth year.
I was told she never stood for photos,
covering her face with her hands
or a scarf, taking the scissors
to any shot that took her by surprise,
excising her face. How did you do it,
you must have been kin, though back then
who could afford a Kodak, who that she knew
would have owned such a car, such a home?
Was this the one time she let you snap

the shutter, stood with her anxious
hands locked behind her back?
Would you remember her now,
as she was then, if we could talk?
I want to believe you were the friend
no one believed she had, someone
lost to family history. I want you
to be the secret she shares
only with me.

In the Time of Flags

It's a long trip, Michigan to New Mexico,
no matter how you make it, and I do each October,
leaving home just as the trees slip
from their frothy summer greens into flame
and harvest hues. I drive south through the palette
of landscape, through the rolling hills of the Ozarks
and plunge through undulations of trees
unfurling autumn for the first frost. This fall,
along Route 54 through Kansas,
the trees seem only to hoard gold,
clumped cottonwoods rich with the sun.

But all along the way there's color
out of season, July's bunting draped over
garage doors and front porch rails, red,
white, and blue arcing in crepe and cloth.
In the heartland there's a flag on every pole,
our country's stars and stripes on pickup glass
and *American Owned and Operated for 27 Years*
declared on the tidy ranch motel.

Forty years ago those colors burned in protest,
smoke rising from scorched fabric
of city streets, anti-war slogans tickling
the flames, Vietnam the flammable fact.

Now Iraq's the tinder. Once again flags burn
in towns around the world so at home
we tout them on everything from football
helmets to packages of hot dogs, dog
collars to ballpoint pens.

My grandmother flew flags of a different kind,
in a garden plot, the lavender-tongued,
lop-eared iris proud on its tough stalk.
She worked her garden in a housedress
and head scarf. Iris unfolded for only
a brief stay, returning to roots to wait out
the hostile months, dividing and doubling
underground. My grandmother's been gone

nearly half a century, but each late May
when the flags unroll, I see her
draped with purpose, bending
over their silky flutter
in old work gloves, rising up,
a rainbow in her arms.

Regarding Skunks

They marched across one of the nine square cubbyholes
in the room divider by the front door, a grinning
mother skunk, ceramic glaze a midnight black,

Milky Way stripe from head to tail, and her three babies,
each about the size of my thumbnail. How they came
to cross that habitat I can't recall. So familiar

they were invisible, I didn't understand why
my cousin, Timmy, a boy raised on the sidewalks
and concrete play yards of LA, loved those baby skunks.

He took them from the mother, whose grin remained
unaltered, and deployed them to the carpet, table,
front porch, and even the pocket of his pj's one summer

night. He fingered them the way I rubbed a pencil,
the way my mother held the thread and needle
under lamplight. He gave them names, and they gave

him connection. One afternoon, as he lined them up
and I shot soldiers on the towers of Fort Apache,
I traded him those skunks for silver dollars, one coin

for every skunk. He spooned them in his palm.
His fingers closed.

What happened next he may remember,
though I don't, until my mother noticed
the childless, though not bereft, remaining

skunk. *Where are those babies?* she inquired
of me either because I was the one most known
for love of furry critters, or because she knew

I was the one most likely in the know if something
went awry. I didn't know, I lied, how could I
know? And yet, when Timmy dredged them

from the pocket of his jeans and rolled them
on the kitchen table, still warm from his body
heat, then said he'd bought them from me

to take home, I lied again, saying I'd rented
them to him for just the day, or just the time
he stayed here in the West Virginia woods.

He knew, my mother knew, but worst of all,
I knew the pain of this exchange. The skunks
returned to mother's care and Timmy took

the silver dollars back home to the West.
I took the scent of skunk. I wear it still.

Ghost House

What went on in that house
my grandmother called home
continues, in some dimension
I can't enter, so that as I stand

wound in brambles and fenced off
by blackberry bushes and a distant
cousin who refuses me entrance
to the dilapidated house

because *it isn't safe,* my grandmother,
as a child, plays with buttons
on the bare floor while upstairs,
my grandmother the betrothed

studies herself in the silver-flecked glass,
runs her finger along the neckline
of her church dress, looks into
her own eyes, unable to imagine leaving

this home for a man, a man who will sink
below the waters of Lake St. Clair,
three states away, before she is twenty-three,
pregnant, with two daughters

she can't yet predict, the unborn one,
my mother, who also stands in the downstairs
parlor surrounded by wallpaper stains,
smelling the dampness of old wood

and shadow, and wondering which room
she should enter next, her hand braced
lightly on the door frame through which I,
as an adolescent, walk with a cousin I loved

and another I envied, into an upstairs room
where we open a seaman's trunk packed
with books, each of us slipping one into our shirts
against parental orders, then walk down

the tight, narrow stairs and out
into the summer light approximately
where I stand now, thirty years later,
with a man I've never met before,

my grandmother's brother's son,
wanting to enter that kitchen
with cracked linoleum and cabinets
peeling decades of paint,

wanting to stand in the stillness clear
as this Mason jar I've salvaged from the weeds,
something left over from canning beans,
putting up peaches, something I turn

in my hands trying to feel heat from the stove
on that August day, what my grandmother
felt that next winter as she brought up,
from the cellar, what she'd preserved.

Remembering My Father, Struggling

The first time he ever said he loved me
was in the middle of a snowstorm.
Carrying my suitcase, he walked me
from the house down the long, slick
driveway to the gravel road where
the VW Beetle huddled, a blue
igloo. I was about to navigate
the icy interstate north to grad school,
to the life I lived without him. He said it
as he stuffed a $20 bill, for gas,
into the unzipped pocket of my parka.
Then he turned and climbed the hill.

The first time I called him on the phone
after they told me about the stroke
and tried to understand his so familiar
voice speaking with an accent never his,
I stood barefoot in shorts and t-shirt
on the cold concrete floor of an artist's studio,
medicinal smells of paint and turpentine
thick as brush strokes on the canvas,
cans on the table filled with brushes
fanned like peacock tails.

Had there been a blizzard in his head,
zero visibility, his van sliding off
some neural highway into an empty field,
no one around to pull him out?
I start to shake as if I might have been
the first one at the scene, though
I know a clerk at Wal-Mart probably
saved his life. I'm afraid

to let him know I can't understand
his speech. I try to answer in a general
way, a *yes,* a *no,* and hope I've got it
right. And then I recognize
the words from long ago, hear them
with as much surprise as I did then,
there on the road when bombarding
snowflakes filled my eyes.
I know the effort saying them requires.

My Mother Recedes into Childhood

I watch my mother become smaller
and smaller as she walks along the lake's
wake toward the lighthouse, a purple
bird pecking the water, looking for
lunch. But she seeks stones,
unusual ones to take home
to Florida, country of translucent
fans and parchment corkscrews,
not chunky granite and quartz
flung up on this northern shore.
She eavesdrops on the conversation
of waves—catching a scrap
of scratched blue glass, a snippet
of leaf a million years old.
She drops them in a plastic pail.
I can make out a boy thumping
against the surf on an unwieldy raft,
two girls with a glittery beach ball,
a school of splashing arms and legs
she wades among, held now
in my memory, forever young.

Sunday Morning on the Carefree Highway

We're headed north out of Phoenix
on the Carefree Highway
toward Carefree, Arizona, my aunt living
with melanoma, my cousin needing
a job, and me, right hand in a splint.
We're going on an *expotition,* my cousin says,
recalling the storybook travels
of that *bear of little brain.* Watching saguaro
punctuate the text of hills like weird exclamation
points, I feel alien in this tale. By the road,
an impromptu flea market with tarps for sale,
wrought iron Kokopellis and coyotes,
and cowboy wreathes make the saga stranger.
It's a Sunday outing for the vendors, too,
kids in the back of parked pickups, a woman
roasting corn in an old drum.
In the backseat, thinking about the comfort
of hugging mountains, the harmony
of red tile roofs, the invisible
cords connecting family, I remember how,
as a child, I liked to draw the dot-to-dots,
turning a page of Dalmatian spots to house,
barn, horse, cow, thinking of the webs
connecting sister to sister, cousin to cousin,
daughter to mother, niece to aunt.

We never see them but they're there,
taut elastic or loose twine, strong as fishing line.
Our Honda hums among a swarm
of Harleys, leather and chrome, rakish and loud.
Oh, my cousin's caught their eye, studs
and silver winking in the sun. She's got a biker boy
back home and loves the ride. I know my aunt
is happy riding with us on this day.
I know the knots are tied.

My Cousin Writes a Letter

for Dan McDonald

the first I've received since that summer
forty years ago when, after a two-week visit,
his family returned to California abandoning me
to my West Virginia self and ordinary friends.
I was thirteen, wedged between wanting
to be Geronimo or the "Venus in Blue Jeans"
Frankie Avalon turned his love to, never sure
one day or the next. He was almost seventeen,
a handsome surfer boy who played the piano
and his grin for me, an older man already
thinking college while I shot baskets
in the netless hoop by the gravel road.
I wrote him a letter the day after he left
telling him where I'd gone to hike,
who won at badminton, how empty
the house was. I didn't mention the echo
in my heart or how many times I'd said
his name that day as if the syllables
could take his shape. He was my worst
teenage crush, the first time I knew
there was space inside my body
for more than anatomy. Always
geographically distant, we've stayed
that way, meeting over the years
at my aunt's house if I drove into town.
Today a dark green envelope arrives,

a thank you for a book of poems I sent
at Christmas, the first gift I've mailed
to him in thirty years. When I slit the seal,
three folded pages lie inside, not a letter
but a poem, an etching of words for this man
who cuts diamonds, lifting light from dark,
carving a thousand prisms into rock.
He retrieves my childhood, smell of leaves
and turtles, taste of cold berries and milk,
wonder of lightning bugs, remembers riding
west to east, then east to west on Route 66,
one lane there, he writes, *one lane back.*
I, toô, have driven America's Highway,
east to west, west to east, and just last year
courted nostalgia through Meramec Caverns,
along the Will Rogers Turnpike, at the Blue Swallow
Motel, in an antique store selling the ice chest
we packed on those 1950s trips and iridescent
tumblers that froze my hand when I drank.
His letter comes along what route I can't say,
narrow envelope tire-tracked with a stamp
from the Old West. I send him this poem
in a white-lined envelope with a postmark
from the automakers' state, his love traveling
one lane here, mine traveling one lane back.

Button Bag

It hunkers in a corner
of my grandmother's closet,
the brown paper soft
as a rag from the rolling,
unrolling and re-rolling
shut. On rainy days
I take it out, hearing
the buttons gossip
when they jostle, sack
scrunched in my arms.
I try to unwrinkle
the red *A&P*.

I dump them
on the linoleum,
careful they don't escape,
wheel under the nubby
sofa or the bench
by the fire,
wobble like bees
down the honeycomb
furnace grate.

They've all been somewhere,
thumbed by someone.

Shoved through
a woolen hole,
slipped from a silk slit.

They could be
nickels
in a dry goods
world, medals
for combat
in kitchen and garden,
stars fallen
from a hounds-tooth sky.

Rhinestones set
in a blue bowl, anchor
etched on a gold sun,
a plaid puff.
Sheriff's badge,
a leather four patch,
this hard metal snap.

They're odd
ones, leftovers,
unmatched like me.

Stalking the Old Neighborhood

I hike up the patched blacktop
that breaks off like a wishbone
from the highway, through foliage
common on all the hills along this river,
come home to walk the old neighborhood,
the one I keep in my head, chaotic
with kids on bikes and fugitive dogs.
Only a few minutes and I pass
the buckeye tree, barren this season,
and the sewer pipe where we tunneled
into the lives of movie heroes. Houses
looking like they've lived here all their lives
clutter the hill where we threw down sleds
and the ravine where the cat had her kittens
rises, swollen like bread. I'm not prepared
for the shrunken yards, hideouts routed
by split level and ranch. There's not a face
I know on any street (there were no streets),
and at the address where my father built
his stone wall, my mother grew her roses,
my brother came late into the family,
and my grandmother died, the huge pines
have vanished like the cousins who
climbed them. It's too hard to take,
all this change, not the old home place

grown over by thicket and vine, squirrels
bickering in the walls, linoleum scrolled up
from the floorboards, but other lives washing
supper dishes in my sink, hanging clothes
on my line, writing letters where I wrote,
keeping their secrets with mine.

Acquisitions

It must've begun with one small treasure
(*button, safety pin, toadstool, acorn*)
I found as I crawled across the floor
or in the grass. Perhaps I stuffed it
in my mouth, or a romper pocket
where it grew lonesome,
needing a friend
(*a nickel, an earring, a carpet tack*),
a companion, a twin.
When I entered first grade
(*new dress, new shoes*),
my mother sewed a sack to hang
from the back of my desk
where I kept the things I was supposed to
(*crayons, paste, pencil, scissors*)
and the things I was not
(*gum, Roy Rogers knife, marbles, fireballs*).
On my trip to California in the second grade,
my Wild West excursion,
(*Stetson, cowboy boots, spear, tomahawk*)
I came home with souvenirs
(*china horses, Chinese finger puzzle, silver dollars*)
to add to the conglomeration
on my bedroom shelf
(*purple monkey, covered wagon, Model T*).

That was before I discovered books
(*The Sugar Creek Gang in School,*
The Sugar Creek Gang in an Indian Cemetery,
The Sugar Creek Gang on a Treasure Hunt)
and later 45's to spin on the turntable
(*Lonesome Town, Tell Laura I Love Her, Dead Man's Curve*)
in a den full of girls in pajamas
eating Fritos and drinking Coca-Cola.
I left for college
(*sheets, towels, laundry basket, textbooks*)
in time to spare my parents
building an addition, a second one.
I moved into McComas Hall
and a life of my own
(*checkbook, address book, date book*).
All that was long ago
(*yearbook, photo album, fraternity pin*)
when my nickname was Rabbit
(*rabbit mug, bunny slippers, hare headband*).
It still is
(*rabbit rain gauge, rabbit mouse pad, rabbit fruit bowl*).
Now I'm looking for a hobby
that takes up little space
(*Pentax, hiking boots, binoculars, bowling ball*)
and requires nothing large

∫

(*printing press, Harley, downhill skis, billiards*).
I want to travel
(*Honda Element, Coleman stove, REI tent, Thule carrier*)
light, with just a pen and notebook
(*computer, printer, collapsible table, thirty cords*),
a knapsack
(*underwear, flashlight, water bottle, matches*),
and a pair of good shoes
(*Birkenstocks, New Balance, Merrill, Tevas*).
I want no maps
(*Rand McNally Atlas, AAA Trip Tik, Interstate Highway
        Guide*),
no cell phone and no credit card
(VISA, MasterCard, Discover, American Express)
ticking like a bomb
in the back pocket of my jeans.

Seductions

BOARDWALK

What I remember:
the bright lights shining
like a heaven of candy
stars as I walked
Daytona Beach,
hands squeezed by my parents.
No constellation
I watched on the hot
summer nights
in West Virginia
where I lay
on a mattress
dragged out to the porch,
a raft in the ocean
of night heat,
could rival these
red blue green gold
flashings of Ferris Wheel,
Shot to the Moon,
Scrambler, and The Swing,
everyone twinkling
to the music of
good times.

CARNIVAL I

The night
of high school graduation
we did not go
to the dance
when our friends,
for the last time together,
lit up the night,
but to the itinerant
carnival parked
at Laidley Field
where for years
cheerleaders
and football heroes
won fame beneath lights.
I could not find
a ride scarier
than tomorrow,
nor music to drown
out the ache,
nor any sideshow
game, despite
the prize, worth
taking the chance.

Carnival II

We all rode
to Princeton
in the back of
a pickup, someone
playing a guitar,
the rest drinking
beer, for a night
at the gypsy fair
wandering the state.
Up, up, and below us
the panorama
of festival,
the music
of jubilee, up
to the top where
our cage spun,
upended,
and falling from
his pocket,
one Winston,
then two, then nickels
and quarters, silver
confetti, wishing
change.

BOARDWALK, AGAIN

This time
it's the off-season,
the storm just passed.
I'm walking by
the Fun House,
House of Mirrors,
house of cards.
Myrtle Beach waits,
an abandoned playhouse,
though funky lights
still squint at
their reflection
in puddles, the calliope
still churns a song
on the wrong speed.
No vendors
hawking foot longs,
no carnies
casting out bait.
I zip my jacket
tighter, remember
my finest Boardwalk:
that elusive blue deed,
the lure of the dice.

Friday Night Singing
at Husky Branch

They've come from all over these hills
with their fiddles and banjoes, mandolins
and guitars, more than the congestion of cars
in the grass where we park. Each room

in the old elementary school is a mini-stage:
a fifteen-year-old piano prodigy in one,
a bluegrass band with female vocalist
and an age seven harmonica player in another,

five guys synchronizing chords, not saying
a word, in a third, and finally, at the end
of the still-smelling-of-school-days hall,
the hymn sing, church pews where desks

used to rest, hymnals on every seat, singers
hollering out *152 now, I said 179, 323?*
while the woman at the upright piano
calls out a key to the men tuning up strings

and off they go. These hymns roll away
fifty years, land me smack in the back row
of Weekley Memorial Evangelical United Brethren
Church where my mother's in the choir loft

giving me that stop-whispering-to-Tommy-evil-eye
look and my daddy's passing the collection plate
and my grandmother's sitting across the aisle
in her good Sunday dress with the other ladies

from the Willing Workers Sunday School Class
flapping their Barlow-Bonsall Funeral Home
fans with the color pictures of The Last Supper
and Jesus in the Garden of Gethsemane

trying to keep the heat from wilting them
like morning glories in the dog days sun.
These aren't the unfamiliar hymns sung
in German at the Mennonite Church in Kansas

I attended when I lived there, or the new
inclusive language contemporary rewrites
I hear in the church in Santa Fe where I go
when I'm in town. The folks here tonight

have come out to rescue the perishing
and lift up the drowning, through song.
They're here to gather at the river, bring
in the sheaves, and get over to glory land.

They want to tell the old, old story
and stand on the firing line for Jesus, you bet.
He's as real in their lives as Wal-Mart
and Lucky Strike. They take us in,

total strangers, (though I hear a lady
across the way say she thinks we're Methodists)
to the fellowship of verse, hymns sung
with a fervor I haven't heard since revivals

and tent meetings where floors were sawdust,
slatted wooden chairs pinched your behind,
and summer night breezes prompted my daddy
to wrap his coat around me as I napped in his lap.

Here the men aren't wearing suits and ties.
The women dress in sweatshirts and slacks.
But tonight I could still be in that back pew
of my West Virginia past, "Just As I Am"

drifting soft and heavy over the shut eyes
of the congregation, everyone humming
the last verse, the last refrain, waiting
for the altar call so we can all go home.

For the Beauty of the Earth

For the wonder of each hour
Of the day and of the night,
Hill and vale and tree and flower,
Sun and moon and stars of light. . . .

—Folliott S. Pierpont/Conrad Kocher

What the Seed Knows

winter plods on like a Russian novel, spring
    hints, haiku

tight blouses unbutton, jackets unzip,
    skin is not just skin

rich soil proliferates
    in the heart, in the hand
    that can never let go

rivers flow unseen, underground, unfettered
    unfathomable

some dig down, some rise up
    some survive

sleep is not dreamless:
    how else the orange, the dogwood?
    the phalanx of asparagus?

coddled in the pod,
    all the seed needs:

darkness, more snug
    than light

∫

grit splits the rock, raises
    a tiny fist, screams
    the world into profusion
    of petaled racket

    to uncurl and unfurl
    to unhusk from the crust

to inhale, exhale
    turn toward what's bright

Bird Watching

for Jesse

Opening the bedroom
drapes these past two weeks,
I've seen you standing
in the sun-sequined grass,
first perfectly still, then rotating,
slowly, slowly, slowly,
your head angled,
looking at the sky.
A cord dangles at your side
attached to binoculars
which you lift
to your eyes
and then turn, turn,
turn again, stopping,
watching, shifting.
From where I stand
I cannot see what
you see: the finch,
the sparrow, a nuthatch,
a chickadee,
and once, you told me,
just once,
an indigo bunting.

At breakfast today
you say you saw a lark
and I, who know nothing
of birds except that
they fly, ask you
how you knew
that's what it was.
You detail the bird,
then gesture how it tilts
its head up,
throws it back.

Several people at the table
follow birds. They share
talk of *plover, purple
martin, pileated woodpecker,
cedar waxwing.*
Waxwings, says our friend
from England, are rare
there.

After grapefruit,
when I walk the road
to the barn,
I'm more aware of chirp

and twitter in the air,
hidden conversation
ten feet high.
Something feathered
jets in front of me, tree
to fencepost, flips his tail
several times in my direction,
lifts his head.
I rule out robin, cardinal,
jay and mourning dove—that much I know.
But now I need
his name, the word
which tells me
we're familiar,
if not family, then
on our way
to being friends.

The Clover Tree

It's been doing this forever, you say,
when I ask you why looking at the water
rushing over stones in Little River makes me cry.
So you must mean something about endurance,
tenacity, the strength to rush ahead through
impossible impediments. *And grace,*
you add, *it's about grace.* I'm lying on my back
on an old quilt pulled from the trunk of your car,
looking up through the leaves of a tree, something
like O'Keeffe must have done before she painted
The Lawrence Tree, but there's no night sky.
You're sitting by the river's edge, close
enough to dangle in your feet, but you don't.
My aunt's name is Grace, I say, being
in associative mode, *and that's one
meaning for my name,* another way
I learned about irony as a clumsy child
who stumbled over air and broke more bottles
of milk than a passel of hungry cats.
You start to sing "Amazing Grace" soft
enough that I can just barely hear it above
the river's song. I remember the first time
I heard you play it on the harmonica, the first time
of many first times, and my friend, dead now
fifteen years, who played and sang that song

the way it was meant to be, a spiritual
conversion. Each time I hear "Good Night, Irene,"
her favorite, tears won't let me swallow.
Wind tumbles in the trees, joining the choir,
when I notice how, without my glasses,
the tree above is a field of four-leaf clover
on this, my lucky day, where I know
what the river knows, and I feel
I could go on doing this
forever.

Corn Maze

after a painting by Linda Hankin

This is no cornfield
I've ever seen though I've lived in the Midwest

half my life, but a seaweedy tangle
of hues, cones of buttery kernels beaming

from anemone husks, alien newborns
incubating in pods. A forest of tassels

steeples skyward. There's a patch of aqua
and eggplant in the lower left, a constellation

of daisies surprising the eye. Walking into
this rhapsody of stalks, these rainbow ribbons

unspooled through the field,
wandering my way through the lattice

of leaves licking the light with cat's tongues,
to turn left, head right, follow the purring

of wind, catch the flicker of fins
and gills disappearing into whiskered grass,

I understand how silence can crackle
into bright silk,

how a story can go on
for a long time.

Zebra Moon

It's the striped effect the moon makes that can be
so disconcerting, as though we had one foot in the
past and one in the present at the same time.
—Margaret Lewis

There will always be a chill
in the air when you recall
this night, a moan
escaping from stone
or stump, the texture of fur
in your hands. There will be
the thump of a spade
breaking the locked earth
and a red amaryllis,
snipped in the kitchen,
bleeding among daffodils
and dirt. There will be the wind,
its language bruised by love,
the syllables swollen and blue.
But above it all, rising
from behind Old Roberts Mountain
like the mirror of your heart's
hole, the moon: the wink
of the lost dog's eye, sometimes
crescent or dozing, then full
and alert to footsteps
on gravel, on guard now
as you return shovel to shed.

Waiting for Snow

On Monday, the weather forecast called
for nine inches of snow, or at least five, and on Tuesday
the clouds gathered stingy and empty-handed.
This is the way it's seemed all winter
though I'm told we're eleven inches over
average for the season. I would have argued
eleven inches under, seeing brown stubble more often
than powder, and limbs unlined with white.
Last night, the Weather Channel lettered
across the screen in disaster orange WINTER STORM
WATCH SUNDAY AM–MONDAY AM.
I went to bed Saturday night, happy
with the day's basketball scores, reading
myself to sleep with a mystery and anticipation
of a morning snow-slung world. When the cat
came in at 5 A.M. to announce our day underway,
it was easy to throw off the covers and get up
knowing that outside, already, the ground
would be several inches soft, the landscape
lumpy and mute. I opened the door
to let him out, warning of high winds and ice
between the claws, then flipped on the light.
He bolted out onto a dry porch, furniture
and log pile recognizable for exactly what they are.

Again I have fallen for the sweet talk
of the Doppler gang, believed I would wake
to a fresh laundry look, clean linen, the outdoors
dressed in Sunday best. I flick on the Weather
Channel, cursing, a total skeptic, see the lime green
Rorschach rolling toward my city's name.
I take my boots from the closet, slam them down
by the door. Once again. Just in case.

Dances on Glaciers

for Lynn Robbins

In early August, we go to Yellowstone
Park, taking Max, half Samoyed,
half standard poodle. At nine months,
he's the size of a small car.
He will grow to the size of a moving van.

We drive the Bear Tooth Highway
to the Top of the World where,
even this late in summer, sheets
of ice shingle the rocks
above Chain Lakes.

We take Max to a stony meadow
by one lake. We're the only ones
there. He splashes in icy water, snaps
at the gurgles in the trickle of stream.

We climb higher and there it is,
a glacier hugging the hillside
(I have just seen *Antarctica* in the IMAX
theater in Portland and know about
the treachery, the deception of sleeping
snow fields).

Max bounds onto the ice,
startled by crystals he kicks up,
takes a bite of the landscape, lunges on.
Up, up the glassy hillside, looking
back, barking for us to come too.

He jumps, huge feet
rising like butterflies, frost flying.
A puff-parkaed boy turns
onto the path.
Dad, a polar bear!
he yells back down the trail.
Max stops, poised
on the glacier's lip, all his weight
twenty feet out over the lake.

He turns, twirls, jubilant
in his cold feet and wet fur,
ice flung from his paws
like diamond confetti,

only himself and snow
in the whole world.

Cat, Bird, Woman

From downstairs, I heard the cry.
A small animal, I thought, something
brought into the house in the cat's mouth.
Too loud for mouse or mole. I know
the rabbit's shriek, the shrill slice
of sound in the air. I'm up the steps,
two at a time, sweeping
the whole room with my eyes.
By the glass doors I see a flash
of red and hear the cry again,
lifting to air, struggling up
amid flapping, then dropping,
then rising, a whirring
like a small fan. Behind the couch
the orange cat takes to the air,
just like the bird, which I now see
is a brilliant cardinal, going up,
slow motion and speed at the same time,
one paw swinging like a prize fighter,
punching the bird's back. As the bird drops,
the cat catches it like a fly ball.
Both land by the window where the cardinal
scuttles into the curtains. I'm beside the cat,
snatch him, carry him to the bedroom

and slam the door. Back by the window
I find the bird huddled in a pile
of loose feathers, still breathing.
I lift it, silk feathers lining
my palm, the heartbeat screaming
in my hand. It doesn't try to fly,
a bad sign, but clamps its orange beak
onto my thumb like a snapping turtle.
The bite is strong. I have to take
my other hand to pry it open.
The bird's legs dangle, the tail's
askew. I think it's too badly injured
to survive, curse the gene in cats
that makes them go after anything
moving, curse the gene in me
that can't bear to watch something die.
I take the bird outside, open my hand.
No wings flutter, but the beak bites down
again, still strong, the black eyes polished
as pain. I take the bird inside,
find a shoe box, tissue paper, cloth
to make a soft bed until it dies.
I take bird and box outside, thinking
to add a nest of straw. When my hand opens,

a combustion of feathers rises,
leaves me wide-eyed in the spring mud
stunned by the miracle of flight.

The Picking Season

First come the blackberries, bushes
ensnared in nettles and bindweed,
the white pine sheltering them
beneath spiky wings. I bring
long-handled clippers to carve
them out of the underbrush, careful
not to cut the canes, not to step
down hard, snap the stalk.
The berries bud green, hard
as hedge apples,
but I know the sweetness
they will grow into.
There's poison ivy everywhere,
but who cares?

Next the cherries explode
from their blossom like July Fourth
fireworks, a starburst here,
a meteor trail there. Birds
discover them, too, taking
one peck at each globe,
assaulting them the way
I did my mother's expensive
truffles and crèmes.
No chocolate on these rubies,

summer's valentine hearts:
tart cherries, tasty
only when congregated
into pies and jams.
Some hug seed and stem,
not ready for plucking, not ready
to leave the cluster, the family
bundle, their only kin.
Others slip easily into my hand,
just the right firmness,
the right plump.

Soon there will be pears,
the tree laden with small fists,
more this year than before,
a neighborhood of foliage
thronged in rebellion.
In time, as with all of us,
they mellow and soften,
age loosening their grip.
Then come the apples,
a profusion of firm spheres
ripening into history:
Nan Nan's pandowdy,
Aunt Bea's fritters,

Aunt Marie's apple
brown betty, Aunt Phyllis's
cobbler, crust mile high
and snow-capped
with hand-churned vanilla.

How lazily we drift through the days
of black suns toward a week
of red planets, then long for
the golden gourd, juicy and cold,
a crisp Jonathan, feisty
from the first bite.
Always, we gather in
more than enough.

What the Cat Brought Home

Here, outside the front door
in 4:00 A.M. porch light, splayed

on its back and gnawed
through its heart,

the frog I've talked with
from our backyard pond, keeper

of secrets and reminder that,
each spring, green things return

to life, camouflaged croaker
of dark's mysteries, proof

that those we love
do not always love what we do,

every purr has fangs, and gifts
can come at terrible cost.

Return of the Bison

My friend says the scrub juniper
in the desert north of Albuquerque
are really buffalo, issued in a new format,
amassing in clumps. Shaggy needles
of green now camouflage the proud heads,
the lethal horns. They have returned
to their ancestral lands, knowing
they need disguise, knowing
if they appear in hide and hoof,
this will not be seen as miraculous.
They will be subject for scrutiny,
then source of revenue.

So they have rooted themselves,
this time, in place, determined to thrive.
Under the rheumy light of the moon,
it is possible to see their eyes glinting
like flint beneath foliage and sometimes
to hear the hissed conversations
of the dispossessed. This morning,
driving from Springer to Clayton,
I see more of the herd come home
to graze. Scraggly and looking a bit
bewildered, big ones, little ones,

fur mangy and unkempt, they drowse
beneath wind-whipped cottonwood.
They sniff the air, eager for thunder.

Stopping by Road on a Summer Morning

Three cars back from the stoplight
near the approach to I-5 South,
in Monday rush hour traffic,
I see a woman in the car ahead,
a black Honda Civic, open
the driver's door and jump out,
bottled water in hand, red hair
in explosion. She leaps up
to the median where a sunflower
droops even more than
sunflowers droop,
green leaves almost grey,
and certainly limp.
She unscrews the cap,
tips the bottle, pours
what's left around the stalk.
As the light turns green,
she bounces back into her car,
makes a left-hand turn,
then another, into my parking
garage. I'm right behind
as she pulls into her assigned
space several-odd numbers down
from mine. I wait for her
to get out, then ask from my rolled-down

window about her stop. She says
she carries water so every time
the light hits red, she has a minute
to hop out, her makeshift garden
hose in hand, and douse the flower.
It seemed a little peaked today,
she muses. *Too much weekend*
exhaust. Although she didn't plant
the flower there, she knows who did.
So now she does her part.
She lifts the empty bottle in salute
or toast before she walks away,
off to fill it for another day.

Psalm Twenty-Three

Out for a Sunday drive, we come upon
a sheep, weed-dining, right on the highway.
You want a photo, so we stop, get out,
cross the road.

Sheep runs. Down the opposite side of the lane.
Toward traffic. Which there is none of. Right now.
We get back in the car, drive off,
skinny-leg sheep jogging

behind us, playing border collie. Oops, car coming.
I flag it: STOP! Sheep stops. Car goes slow.
You snap. Sheep turns, turns again. Follows. Us.
I pull off the road, get out, go to the gate:

Tied. Wired. Locked. Sheep watches. I watch
sheep approaching the gate, inside the fence.
Twenty eyes in Russian fur, matador hats. All halt.
I untie a rope, lean hard, shoulder the next gate open.

Sheep retreat. Sheep advance:
Elastic sheep. Sheep talk to sheep. I talk to sheep.
Sheep bleats. You snap. Sheep bolts toward
wad of fleece. I bolt the iron gate. Sheep now behind bars.

Goodness and mercy, Lord. Pasture and stream.
Done with wanting. All is restored.

Vocabulary Night

I would like a list of words for every star:
    cataclysm, vertiginous, forever, grief.
I would like such words to hang
as easily in the lunar spaces of my brain
as these stars I walk beneath tonight,
my feet sloshing through one puddle,
then another, splashing
in a red dirt Milky Way. I refuse
to bring artificial light to this holy path.

I wish words to burn as bright
in their constellations—
    story, poem, prayer, song—
    as these heavenly trinkets of the dark,
to periodically flash
by as they explode, disperse
into cosmic matter, caught
in the rear view eye of only the most astute.

I want words to yap
in the gut language
of coyote. I want other words
to yip back. I want to feel as safe
with words as I do wandering
among these desert intimacies.

I ask the stars to tell me all
they know (*rock, spear, rifle, bomb*)
about human choice, about how
we got it wrong, to offer an antidote:
    hand, cup, bread, gift.

I give thanks for the stuff of legend—
    Orion, Castor, Pollux, Ursas Major and Minor—on
    the blackest nights, for the warmth
of a quilt of sequined cloth:
Morning Star, Star of Bethlehem, Lone Star, Broken Star.
And for a night lit by the candle power
of quasar, red dwarf, white giant, pulsar,
language I will never understand.

Lord, make each word a star, each star a word:
    hoodoo, Appalachian, Alzheimer's, hymn.

Love Lifted Me

Love lifted me!. . . .

even me!

Love lifted me!. . . .

even me!

When nothing else could help

Love lifted me.

—James Rowe/Howard Smith

Hunger

In the room where I sleep
alone, the message of your hands

draws me like light, its fingers
opening the tight petals

of eyes, of lips, picking
this locked syntax of need.

The message breaks like bread.
It is never enough.

No Apostrophe Needed

for Dr. J. B. Shrewsbury

I never told you how you changed
my life that November afternoon in your small
office, walls lined with bookshelves, shelves
lined with Dickens, Hardy, Carlyle
and others all we English majors groaned
over because they were so stuffed with words
and anguish we had no time for, took too long
to read when we had football games and dances,
washtubs of Purple Passion on the banks
of Brush Creek, and certainly more to do
than ponder the fate of Tess and Angel Clare,
though some of us would have been wise
to pay attention here. I had a boy then, too,
tall and blonde, blue-eyed behind his scholar's
lenses, though he had already begun to give up
formulas and themes for the camaraderie
of brothers and bottles at The Tilt, named
for its precarious perch on the coal-seamed
mountain. When you closed your office door
behind us, you seemed nervous, as was I,
of course. I think what might have happened,
knowing what I do now from being the professor
you were then, what students tell me about
seduction and bad judgment in the name of help.
Don't marry him, you said, and I was floored,

never having spoken to you before about anything
but trees of derivation, objective correlatives,
and rules of grammar I was inclined to break.
You had other plans for me, which had no place
for him, nor you, as an observer might suspect.
Go on to school, you told me, stay out of small town
English classes, do something more than spend
days diagramming sentences, nights waiting
for someone who's not coming home.
Don't worry where he's been,
nor who he's with. On your desk I saw
a book of Matthew Arnold's poems.
Not all love finds us on a darkling plain.
In that room you showed what might be
mine. So now, this poem is yours.

Sleeping with Rilke

It's not what you think.

I am not a young poet to whom
he writes passionate letters toying with
syllables or secrets only the two of us
possess. If we had been intimate
in these ways, he might have shared
a mole with me or left a snapped-neck
dove outside the bedroom door.
His use for feathers is unrelated
to quills.

Still, I had to visit several times
before we shared a bed,
before he let his body curve
to my hand. In return, he touched
my face like the memory of touch,
only the suggestion of love.

It was I who flipped off the light, hoping
he would not take flight.
In the dark of an unfamiliar room
I felt his weight settle into my side,
his back press into the small of my back,
a proposal for the possible.

He curls in the arc of my knees.
He murmurs his latest verse,
purring us to sleep.

How Bodies Fit

In outer space, they orbit, each
keeping its perfect and known distance
from the other, except for renegade
stars which shoot off this way and that
like startled cats. Or on land, think about
the Great Lakes, the way three of them
rendezvous near the Soo, the other two
excluded by Detroit. Think how the body
of the essay slips cleanly between
introduction and conclusion, transitional
sentences tucking it in, or a baseball
snuggles in the soft pocket of glove.
And those six puppies,
see them tumble together in the plastic basket
like lumpy laundry, one brown head poking
through two mismatched paws, seamless
in their reconfigured selves. Or us,
at night in the lull of sleep,
how leg migrates toward leg,
the shifting of tectonic limbs, knee
nudging knee, wave to shoreline,
two islands reunited
after years adrift.

Drought

It's been a full year, almost to the day,
without poems, my mouth parched
from the dearth of words, pages
lacking vegetation, nothing grown
from the few scattered seeds.
The days burn white. Nights
struggle for air. The stars
that spark the lyrics of my heart
languish under clouds. I listen
for a sign the wind is up, the scent
of memory blowing in: a fish
flickering in a pool, aquamarine
and flame ripped through the evening
sky, a sheep skull glinting in dewy grass.
The door opening and, standing there,
you, drenched with rain.

Among the Boats

splashing at play in Sarasota Bay, my brother's red
and white speedboat (is that what it's called?) romps

across the wake of larger boats, a rabbit
in a fluid blue meadow of rambunctious pups.

He darts between a modern galleon flying the flag
from *Camelot* and a cruiser hovering like the QE II

above his rascal loose in the company of the elite.
I just smile at them and wave, he laughs,

and lifts an eyebrow, adding, *Mine's paid for.*
As his boat's nose goes down for a dive, a tsunami

rises over the bow where his daughter and my father
doze, sunstruck lizards on a rock. Water smacks

the prow like an irate batter, the two of them dumped
to the deck, wide-eyed and dripping like laundry.

I am looking behind at the choir of sailboats tilting
to the music of the sea, the effortlessness

of their breathing, the way they are the waves
that lift them, nodding to yachts and Jet Skis, so lovely

they are almost illusion, lovers I had but didn't have,
notes of that thought-forgotten song

that always catches me off guard.

Woman with Something to Say

I would not have loved you
if not for the green waves of the hills
we sang our way along,
the music of rain an undertow.

If not for the green waves of the hills
I could not have heard the song,
the music of rain an undertow,
your words, notes caught in the curl.

I could not have heard the song
I gave myself in darkness, in fact.
Your words, notes caught in the curl
in creek beds, turned to frolic.

I gave myself in darkness, in fact.
We dove for stars, fished for light
in creek beds, turned to frolic.
When you vanished, I swam back.

We dove for stars, fished for light.
We burned resplendent just before explosion.
When you vanished, I swam back,
despite it all. It seems absurd to write.

We burned resplendent just before explosion.
We sang our way along.
Despite it all, it seems absurd to write
I would not have loved you.

On Vicki's Porch

We called it *the stoop,* a concrete
slab beneath the back door,
two steps down to the ground.
I sat there in the bee-humming
thick of summer. Sniffing
the air for rain. Listening for tires
chewing up dirt. Watching
wooly worms hump across rocks.
My daddy painted the stoop green,
then, years later, brick red. In August
the stoop was a hot coal.

 This May we sit in wicker chairs
 on Vicki's curved porch, in the crook
 of its arm. This is the porch
 of Southern lore, Victorian veranda
 open to Lake Michigan, vacation
 folk from Chicago clinking cold drinks.
 But we're in Kansas, already a sea of heat.
 Old friends gather here for chat.
 Some crackers, a few glasses of wine,
 salted nuts, a bowl of fruit. One red apple
 on a glass plate, two strawberries touching.
 There's a tornado gusting from the west
 but we don't know it yet, one that will be

headline news. The grass in the yard
murmurs, talk of the entwined.
Across the street, a dog hops on his igloo
doghouse like a circus dog on a ball.
But he's going nowhere, barking. A car
goes by, honks the horn. *It's David,*
someone says. Another says she's writing
about hope, attempting to prove it doesn't exist.
One of us has survived an aneurism.
One this day gets a diagnosis: Parkinson's.
One of us wants her life to change. Another
believes it will. Two of us live four states away.
It's been years since we've all been together.
The porch shimmers, a constellation
harboring stars, a song learning its own notes.
The wind sings one tune we all know.

I sang to myself on the stoop.
I pulled my knee against my chest
and rocked, imagining the days
ahead, inventing words
I needed, letting warmth seep
up into my body, radiating like a stone.

At the Winery

This used to be an orchard,
and before that, hills where the same
hardwoods lodged for generations.
Then came the fire, charcoal soil
making the land ripe for planting,
for staking the vines in rows uniform
as markers in a military cemetery.
We come this morning with four dogs
to hike the trails beyond the grapes.
All senior citizens, by some chronologies,
we come as much for the spirit
as health of the body. We've known
each other nearly forty years,
an unimaginable span.

The sun is out, the air cool. We start
up the trail, the little Jack Russells,
Tatoo and Kazoo, maniacal for the lead,
wind-up toys with only one speed.
Freeda, the apricot Husky, comes next,
then Buck, part Wolfhound, part Brillo pad,
part polish sausage. When he was a pup.
someone dubbed him a Jack Russell
because of his face, before he weighed
ninety pounds. We're into the woods

now. Twigs snap under foot. Light splashes
on quartz and Nelson County granite.
The blooms of paulownia burst
overhead like lavender flares.
I bend back a sassafras, remember
my grandmother brewing tea from the root.
We have a map, drawn on a paper sack,
to guide us to the top and back,
though there's disagreement among us
when we come to the orange tape
stretched across the path as if it's a crime
scene: Stop here? Go up? Go down?

Return now? Never a trio to turn back,
we go on instinct, like the dogs,
and head south. We cross a stream
where Kazoo decides to lie down,
Freeda to snorkel. Buck drinks.
Then we're snared by thorns, besieged
by ticks. Dogs belly-slide under fallen trees,
we climb over. We reach the deer fence,
see a metal roof glinting
beyond the wire.

It's been exertion for us all,

except the Jack Russells, frenetic
as ever. In a novel I just read
one of the doomed characters trains
dogs to be messengers during WW I.
His favorite's a Jack Russell, heroic
as any combatant, zigzagging bullets
and mortars to ferry words from the front:
Send more ammo. Casualties mounting.
It's no war zone here this morning,
though in other parts of the world bombs
detonate and casualties still rise.
Here, only wine ferments in the casks,
only grapes burst their ruby skins.

In Praise of Forgetfulness

What if my aunt, from the always-brand-new moment
of her illness, asks me if it's snowing in Michigan
six times in the first two minutes of our weekly
call and, what if, each time I say, *Yes,*
we have half a foot and it's still coming down?
What if all of what we can't remember
floats in our snow globe brains
like downy flickerings
drifting to a new terrain each time
our world's turned upside down?
If I don't find the car keys, possibly
it's time to walk. If I lose the digits
in your phone number, perhaps a letter
should go in the mail. I remember
the little lady in the care home
who, when I forgot her name and apologized
for doing so, laughed and touched
her fingertips to cheeks, as if to test
if she were really there, then said
I shouldn't worry, since often she can't
remember who she is. Or was.
When the time comes
that you're a stranger to me
every day, let me love meeting you

each time with that same leap of heart
and hope of what's ahead that I remember.
I praise the music, praise the coming storm.

School Physiology *Exam: 1880*

1. What is the shape of the heart? What is its position in
   the chest?

   The heart is clay, shaped by the hand that turns it.
   A fish growing to the size of its pond.
   Liquid rising in the cup of love.
   It leans neither to the left nor the right.
   It is neither Democrat nor Republican.
   But it is pro-choice.

2. How many cavities are in the interior of the heart?

   More than you think.
   More than it counts.
   One for each loss.
   Stalactites and stalagmites link arms in the dark.

3. To what are the regular movements of the heart due?

   To the cannons of war.
   To the wonder of song.
   To the ring of a phone.
   To the cadence of a poem.
   To the curl of smoke.
   To the breaking of light.

4. Where is the beat of the heart felt?

Against the taut drum of anger.
In the mixer of jealousy.
Through the fists of despair.
On the drenched canopy of affection.

5. Which side of the heart has the most labor to perform?

The side which, at that moment, hungers.

6. What is the impulse of the heart?

Electrical, like a storm.

7. What effect has sex on the size of the heart?

In men, it always wants to be larger.
In women, it seeks to be stronger.

8. How is the heart covered?

It is not.
No insurance company in its right mind would take
the risk.

9. Does the heart have any rest from labor?

> *Does the sun stop shining when we don't see it?*
> *Will time stop if we smash the clock?*
> *Can passion ebb if we beg it?*

10. What is the organ of touch?

> *By now, you know it's not my hand.*

Eleven Months Later

There is no poem in my work, no story
unfolding, lovely as the calla lily.

Instead I lumber through days, then months
beneath a canopy of darkness, in a season of rain.

Then, a newspaper arrives with the hesitant dawn.

I see the sky has turned tornado-green.
I count the number of twigs stirring, scribbling

on the window, listen for tires
inscribing lines on the red clay driveway.

I imagine the imprint of your feet
on the new spring grass.

Already I feel your hip lean
into the front door, push it open.

You say my name.

Retreat

Back to the hills, the old worn ones,
flannelled with deciduous green, stitched
together by Schuylkill, Rappahannock, Kanawha,
Monongahela, Shenandoah, Susquehanna.

Back to the farmhouse, hand-hewn
beams, wide plank floor. Aroma
of smoked ham hung in the kitchen.
Names swapped at the table.

Ask: what do I know
I'm not telling? Where is the photo
you took by the river? That foot-shaped rock,
the box of moth wing letters, the medal
won in the war? What am I telling
I don't know?

Find the brambled trail. Stop
by the pond where bullfrogs break open
the night. The overturned canoe,
the ramshackled shed: shovel, rake,
simple tools of work. Pencil stub
on a two-by-four. Cobwebs
curtain a broken window, something

scuttles from the light. What's in the corner,
behind the wheelbarrow?

Into silence. Into the attic
of stored days, the damp cellar
of the heart.
Into the conversation
that might never have happened.
Hear the echoes,
still?

But Not Forgiving Myself

I am forgiving my grandmother for dying
before I was smart enough to pester her
about my grandfather, drowned trying
to save another man, before I had courage
enough to step into silence, before I was alive
long enough to appreciate death.
I am forgiving my brother for being born
only four months after my grandmother died,
for confiscating her room where, still,
at night I could hear her terminal cries,
for being the boy my father always wanted
when I was the girl who always wanted
to be a boy.
I am forgiving the boy next door
for what he asked me to trade for cinnamons
wrapped in crinkled cellophane and butterscotch
suns that turned out to bring the dark of night.
I am forgiving the night
for its currency of stars, for its coin
of cold white light I have put myself in debt
with, for the way it has allowed me
safety, and the undressing of love.
And, finally, I am forgiving love
for finding me, for then not finding me,

for abandoning me, for misunderstanding me,
for kicking me hard when I was already
down, and finally, finally,
for loving me.

Let the Lower Lights Be Burning

Trim your feeble lamp, my brother,
Some poor sailor tempest tossed,
Trying now to make the harbor,
In the darkness may be lost.

—P. P. Bliss

From the Lighthouse

for Vicki Stamp

When I lived in your state, I drove
those endless plumb line roads from east to west,
and, in summer, cut through the swell
of curling wheat, the only car in sight, lulled
to boredom by silence and heat.
Once I saw a car, its driver mesmerized
in this same way, run a stop sign, broadside
a pickup carrying German Mennonites
on their way home from church.
Though the camper back was flattened
and three children spared, those in the cab
were sliced by windshield glass
and nearly died. I puzzled how,
in all this open space, the two
were drawn like magnets to collision.
In my home state, cars crash head-on
trying to pass on hairpin turns
in dusky twilight, or risk crack-up
blinded by snow. I learned early
if I saw a beam of light not to cross
the center line. No lighthouse flashed
a beacon to drivers navigating the crest
on Mink Shoals hill, the old Athens-Princeton
narrows, the tricky straits of Hawk's Nest.
In Green Bank, a towering radio telescope

aims to pick up word from distant stars,
remains closemouthed to travelers
reckless on mountain roads. Here in Kansas,
grain elevators rise above the waves
of wheat, silent as the Sphinx
toward all around them.
No light pulses from these pillars, no alert
sails out into the treacherous calm.

Cause and Effect

All morning the dark clouds assembled
to the east, banging their angry fists
against the blue window of sky,
flinging rain among trees
like shattered glass.
In my upstairs room I typed on,
striking each key like a bad memory
sent packing, assaulted letters
cowering into words.
Too much water, too much
weight. Thunder in the sky, thunder
on the page and in the midst of it,
crack of the big birch
snapping at the base, crashing
through hemlock and maple
like a white swell, a twister
of bark, a truck driven at high speed
into rock. Then silence
as it lay broken, a prehistoric femur,
blocking the road. The life
of trees, the life of words, the unexpected
rip through the forest, the letter falling,
still folded, from its white sleeve,
stopping us cold.

Oklahoma Family Portrait, 1928

Here is the family, lined up
like fence posts in the cotton field
for some itinerant photographer
with a black box and a silver tongue.
They're all studying the camera,
faces void as the bank account,
except for the small boy who
has turned his back to the lens.
He's looking behind at something
we can't see just as the shutter snaps,
his face lost forever to history.
What is it that makes him turn
just now? Does he hear the wild stallion
of his dreams stampeding by, fear
the gunshot his father, this man
in the sombrero to his left,
is said to have fired at one,
bringing it to its knees?
Has he heard the horse's cry
or the silence that follows?
When he finally turns back
to face the lens, already too late,
will we see what knowledge
he's acquired? The woman
stands to the right, her hand

on an older girl's shoulder,
driving her into the earth.
Unlike the boy, the girl
has her eyes nailed
to the man with the tripod,
fists clenched at her side,
having already learned the cost
of distraction, the price for imagining
the moonlight yipping of the coyote
to be anything but noise.

The Visitor

4:00 A.M. and the new kitten purrs
into the bedroom from an outlying
district, jumps to the comforter,
motors north through the blue ridges
toward the hills of pillow.
I sense him coming, vibrations
rocking the room, ready
for the jolt of his wet nose,
spider-leg whiskers, and the curl
of his supple body against my face.
He leans into my breath.
Not content for long, he migrates
behind my head, wraps a feline muffler
about my neck, then settles on my chest,
a hood ornament from the 1940s,
a little furnace, motor running
all the while. It's impossible to sleep.
When the radio plays, he bounds
away to hunt the house's other cat.
The phantom weight of muscle
stalls on my chest, over my heart,
reminding me of love that settles in,
then leaps away, leaving all that
fisted energy, that invisible freight.

Losing My Hands

Always it's the comment:
*I never thought this would happen
to me.* A friend comes home
from a routine exam, her life shortened
by decades. My father, from his hospital
bed, tells me he was just standing in line,
just waiting to pay at the checkout
and, suddenly, there was no sound.
My cousin, the biker, says she never
saw them. Never. My mother says
that was the one day the dog
jumped the fence.

All my life I've built things:
Lincoln Logs and Tinker Toys
or a stone wall in the side yard.
I've thrown balls through hoops
and windows, I've written page
after page in this notebook, graded
more papers than acorns fallen
in fall. I've painted streams
curling through watercolor fields.
I've painted walls. I've poured
tea, pitchers of beer, concrete.
I've stitched ripped seams

and wounds, ironed my shirts
and my hair, washed the dishes
and the dog. I had not thought
how thumb presses against forefinger
to guide the pen or how the wrist
flexes easily to lift the cup,
how fingers wrap themselves
around the cord on the chainsaw.
I've taken for granted the clipping
of clothespins, the lifting of skillet,
the gripping of racket.

Now I know what a gift this is,
the turning of knobs, the clicking
of keyboard, that finger and thumb
aren't always close kin, that shock
can surge through the wrist, that parts
of the body can refuse to do what
they're told. So hard to imagine
a life of unlifted lids, of unscrewed
screws. I remember when my father,
after that stroke, had to call my brother
to hold nails and my friend with Parkinson's
wasn't steady enough to sign checks.

How sad, I thought,
and went on playing my guitar.

In August, my guitar was stolen
from my truck, a smashed window
the only evidence of the theft.
No torturer has broken bones in my hands
nor have I had thumbs pulled
from their sockets by force.
No one has wired me with electric
current nor taken a cleaver to my wrist.
But pain is a strange thing breaking
into a life, coming when it's ready,
taking what it wants. The house
is never the same again, inhabited
always by phantoms, the owner
still bewildered this could happen
to her.

The Building Trades

You kneel on my porch, say you're tired
of that loose board, every *thwack*
with the hammer announcing an old grief,
a hard loss. You have built your way
through disaster: a deck when the woman
you loved phoned to say she was releasing you
to your own life; a hickory kitchen
when your father had his first stroke;
a window seat after the cat had been gone
six months. When I hear the pound, pound,
pound of metal against pine, I wonder
what it is this time that's driven you
to the harbor of post and beam,
the chapel of rafter and ladder?
When you offered to replace the railing
tilting north like the hypotenuse
of a triangle, I knew your silence
was working its way out, the pain
diminishing with each stroke and blow.
I, too, have need of nails,
though I'm the kind more likely to claw
them out of solid planks, my anger
prying into soft wood
like a neighbor who will not
let it be, will not stop asking who

it was departed my house
last night at 2:00 A.M., who
will not step back from the curtain
even when the porch light
goes dark.

Double Valentine

At sixty, my grandmother died
surrounded by three daughters
while I slept, unaware,
on a couch in another room.
You're sixty today, unaware
I'm thinking of you,
about how it is possible
for you to be that age.
A grandmother, too,
and mother of three,
you're surrounded by dogs
and CDs, watercolor tubes,
friends to sing you into
the next decade, not by pills,
a bedpan, a new piano
gathering dust. She died
in the month you were born,
borne away in a blizzard
right out of a Russian film.
I don't know what weather
brought you into life, only
what weather you brought
into mine. The war was on,
chaos around you, at best.
Snow's in today's forecast,

enough to soften stumps
and rocks, cloak the pines.
I loved you both, never
making the connection
until now, how the heart
goes dormant in a season
of cold, how blood
hungers to blossom.

Father and Daughter
at the Nursing Home

We're visitors, thank God, here to see a woman
who doesn't know us, who barely knows
her daughter of more than fifty years.
It's a puzzle to me how the mind gives
way like old floorboards, first a little
creak of warning, then collapse,
crashing sanity into the musty
root cellar of remembering, walls
dank, dirt damp, space dark.
Something familiar here, we say,
but what? My father, eighty-two,
the same age as the woman we visit,
must wonder how it is he still knows
his children's names, can balance a checkbook,
find his way to the grocery store. And back.
He'd say, *Golf!,* his glue for keeping
all the stones in place. I watch him talk
with her as though she could tell him
if she likes the food or wants to go outdoors.
Feeling her paralysis, he switches gears,
tells her about the town in Florida
where he lives, my mother's convalescence
from a broken hip, snow that's the first
he's seen in twenty years. I watch him
coax so hard for what she might offer

I can't speak for fear of tears.
We're in a basement room, lighting
poor, the TV show disjointed as her thought.
Somewhere outside, no window here,
a train lurches by. How he must pray
not to find himself some day in a place
like this, me in the chair beside him
jabbering a language he can't speak as
golf ball, Bible, soldier, wife line up,
empty boxcars on a derailed train.

The Return

for Andre Watts

Could it have been the William Tell
you heard that night the blood
clot exploded through your veins,
a cannonball targeting
your brain, knocking you
flat? Or was it the mad
Beethoven pounding as if he needed
sound to breathe, not air?
I imagine what chords
I might have heard, raised
on hymns, not sonatas
or symphonies, the revival tent
swelling with "Love Lifted Me,"
voices by the river offering
"Power in the Blood,"
"Onward Christian Soldiers"
concluding the funeral of a good friend.
Could it have been Wagner
setting ablaze the Nordic night
you heard, keys burning like white
torches? Your wife writes
that you are home, sleeping now,
borne across the country
in three hours' time. She says
your first gesture upon return

was to touch the piano (Brahms,
she writes). I see you fit
your fingers to the keys the way,
after near disaster, we touch
a face we love, hardly believing
we could be so lucky,
still together in the same life.

Psalm for Anne

Thou art my hiding place, thou
shalt preserve me from trouble;
thou shalt compass me about
with songs of deliverance.

—*Psalm 32:7*

Here we are, at breakfast
in this sunlit restaurant,
professors going over notes
on our left, two co-eds laughing
and spilling coffee on our right.
We order eggs, Spring Omelets,
the menu says, with asparagus
and tomato, red and green
of Christmas or confetti.
But this is no celebration.
You've come to talk about
the tumors in your liver,
news of metastasis,
heartbreak the day you left
for good your job in the library.
Your partner sits across the table
calmly eating pancakes.
Later, I notice she carves
a face into the one remaining.
We could be discussing what you might
say in my class next term to make

the students love learning like you do,
or a novel you've read you say
I must, too. I can't take it in
that we're talking of your death,
those leaving and those left behind.
Last night in a dream my best friend,
dead ten years, gave me the keys
to her house, and though it was winter,
and I didn't want to go, I did.

From the window I could see the ice
on Lake Michigan growing like stalagmites,
but the room was bright, warm, familiar,
where I'd been with a former lover.
So you're here telling me the arrangements
with the funeral home, the difficulty
of plans for cremation, in the same voice
you talk about how it took you nine hours
once to meander home from Grand Rapids
to Lansing, you loved the journey so.
It's clear to me now the reason
for last night's dream: pay attention,
my always-mentor friend was saying,
you'll come to this cottage, too.
But I will have watched you pack

for the trip, watched you choose what to take,
to leave behind, needing neither anger
nor grief, have heard you say how,
though your mind always wanders
during sermons, now as you read Psalms,
the language of some passages seems
absolutely luminous. When we part
in the parking garage, you climb
stairs to your car on the level above.
I'm on my way downtown,
taxes to be filed, hoping
not to be audited this year.

Girls Crossing Over

Driving west across Iowa, humdrum
clouds slumped over green fields,
I'm tuned to *Talk of the Town* on NPR,
listeners calling in about abducted children.

A father whose son vanished
in a parking lot twenty years ago,
parts of his body found in a canal
three weeks later, shares his loss.

On the other side, there's a man
who stole his daughter from his ex-wife,
because of the boyfriend, he says,
then lit out for Mexico.

The next caller asks, *What do I tell*
my twelve-year-old to keep her
safe? I think how vulnerable
we all are, parents and children alike,

how the fluke moment stuns
us, remember James Bulger,
the two-year-old, his ten-year-old
killers who, after serving nine years,

secured release this week. The sky
lowers, smothering barn and silo.
Ahead I see an overpass, something
moving at the rail so I slow down,

recalling the story several years ago
of kids dropping bricks on autos
from a bridge, at least one woman
killed. Since few cars travel my side

of the road I have time for a good look:
three young girls, maybe ten or twelve,
lean out over the highway, waving,
eager to catch my eye, inviting

a wave back. I raise my hand,
grateful for innocence still
loose in the world, unnerved
when I think who sees it.

Trouble in the House

I didn't see her body,
loosely clothed, lying oblivious
as the room was doused,
the match struck.

I didn't come
into the house till two days later,
asked to help inventory
the waterlogged wardrobe,
exploded televisions, odd items:
scattered personal papers including
a notice of payment in arrears,
almost $4,000 for child support;
a disposable camera; a box of small bottles
of beer salt; three high school yearbooks,
inscriptions written to someone
I never knew.

Hours later my eyes still burned,
and though the fire was snuffed out
shortly after it erupted, I still
carry the image of the burned mattress,
melted plumbing, charred walls,
children's toys scattered in the debris.

Once, in a police station,
I was asked to read a letter
a killer sent detectives detailing
his crime. I was asked about grammar
and syntax, as though I could ignore
the hanging of the victim while I looked
for inconsistency among dangling participles.

I couldn't sleep for days, though
no odor clung to me. My eyes
stung, but not from fumes.

I still feel smoke lining
my throat, see soot streaking the walls
in the room where she died,
and though I never heard the gunshots
the neighbors say they heard,
I hear the scuffle that takes place

this morning in my bathroom,
the cat bringing in his first catch
of the season, a fat robin,
find feathers littering
the tile, swatches of blood
on the white wall, and the bird

huddled beneath the pipes
behind the toilet, not knowing

if my hand, darkness
closing around him,
means doom
or chance,
the way out.

A Matter of Perspective

All the parents are failing. Last week,
word came of a mother in Richmond,
confined in Alzheimer's, now squeezed
by double pneumonia, and today,
a daughter calls to say her mother's moved
to hospice, too much chaos at home,
too many responsibilities for her last days.
On my e-mail screen I find a note from a friend
in D.C. saying her father's struck down
by congestive heart failure for the final time.
The sisters have all come, the mother's unable
to believe he will not rise again. Melanoma
spreads through the blood of my aunt in Phoenix,
my cousin in the air now on her way there.
It's epidemic. *We're at that age,* we all say,
looking down.

My own parents came for Christmas,
my father abandoning his Florida greens
for ten days of snow, my mother
resistant, swaddled in blankets
by the fire. He's fending off age with golf clubs
and hammers, learning to add memory
to his computer, flying across the country
to military reunions. He will not be taken

without a fight, this man shot twice in The War.
My mother reads, doesn't go out much since
she broke her hip. When I take them to the Detroit
airport to fly south, we suffer lost baggage tickets,
misplaced boarding passes during security
check. My mother loses her ID, which turns up,
after great search, in my father's pocket.

I persuade the woman at the desk to let me go
with them to the gate, my father hard of hearing,
my mother tucked in a wheelchair. We have coffee
waiting for their call to board, then I hustle them
forward when the attendant announces pre-boarding
for those with platinum cards or special needs.
We hug, then my father hunches over the wheelchair,
pushes off toward the ramp. I watch them shrink
from sight. I say a prayer to help them home,
since I cannot. All the children are failing.

When the Moon Slipped Loose
of the Sky like a Button Undone

There is no poetry on this long road south.
Fields grow sickly with winter, trees skeletons
of their summer selves. Once I found sonnets
on this ten-hour trip, and a limerick rhyming
Wapakoneta with *cannot forget 'cha,*
haiku where syllables met: *the strand of pearls*
my lover brings me tonight, such exquisite moons.
A train shuffles by headed the wrong way.

I sail past the concrete moon rising
from the concrete earth at Exit 113, think
of that first man to kick his boot in lunar dust,
knocking the moon from myth to fact.
Here's fact: I'm shipwrecked on this highway
though I've no boat and water's miles away.

Sweet Hour
of Prayer

In seasons of distress and grief,
My soul has often found relief,
And oft escaped the tempter's snare,
By thy return, sweet hour of prayer.

—Catherine Hankey/William C. Fischer

Road Song

You and I, my friend
of more than half our lives,
rolling along the Blue Ridge
Parkway laughing like thunder
lost in a snowstorm, the old
green truck loaded with enough
stories to make us
Tales-on-Wheels,
rain slapping the windshield
in an offhand gesture
of affection
and the sun,
that genius child
who pops into the conversation
at the moment
you never expect,
reminding us how
trees have their own outbursts
of joy
and the dark red earth
can be stunning
as any sunset.

Grief

It's always related to travel.
Someone going one way.

Someone else another.
Sometimes literal, sometimes

metaphorical: it's the interstate
with no exits or rest stops.

Definitely no motels. A deer lies
dead on the roadside, legs

extended in a final
and permanent leap.

It's the old home place
they took you to in childhood,

wide porches for sitting and talk,
stone hearth for supper and warmth.

You could have cared less then,
but now, now the highway

no longer runs there, no one's
alive with the map in her head.

Now all that matters is finding
that house, the road to it

hidden on someone else's land.
Always someone else's land.

Looking for the Name of God

for Talitha Arnold

It's not like shopping, looking
for the lowest price, the best bargain,
the size that fits, the perfect gift.
It's not the quest for something lost.
It's not looking for trouble
nor looking out for the little brother
you'd like to leave behind. It may be
closer to looking for the cure
for the common cold. So simple,
if only we could get the first clue.
It's not like finding a name
for the new puppy, or the name
of a street in a foreign town.
Naming God is not the same
as *Name that Tune.* It's not looking
for that pot of gold at rainbow's end
nor the prize in the Cracker Jacks.
It's not looking for the name
in the phone book, on the best-
seller list, on the dotted line.
The name of God is not
a noun (a person, place, or thing)
but a verb (an action word).
It is the looking that's the name of God.

House of the Rising Sun

There's a church in the valley by the wildwood,
No lovelier place in the vale.
No spot is so dear to my childhood
As the little brown church in the dale.
—Traditional hymn

In the years of starched white crinolines
inflating my skirt like a hot air balloon,
white gloves, and hats of pastel straw,
the ritual of Sunday morning came predictable
as the tides. There were polished patent leathers,
thin socks with scalloped tops, and no gum.
There was the ride to church in the Ford,
whatever model, and the same parking space
in the bank lot. Arrival 9:25. This was no
country church, but stucco walls high
like Jericho, rising among old frame houses,
Joshua somewhere in the next block.
I remember a porch on the same street where,
in warm weather, a man in a sleeveless undershirt
sat reading the Sunday *Gazette*. What was it like,
I wondered, the life of someone who did not go
to church, who had Sunday morning free to do
the unimagined? Inside the sanctuary smelling
of coolness and waxed wood, the preacher
droned on, his tone keeping me wary.
His fury made me wonder who could love

his God. Behind him, the green-robed choir
sprang up like a forest when the director
gave the sign, scrunching in together
as if posing for a photo, black books opened,
shared in twos. They sang of gardens,
rocks, the sea, a different church
in a different place. I did not sing
in my voice of sheep bleats, wooly
around the high notes, the sheep
that was lost. But their voices
chimed with light. I remember
how the sun struck the stained glass
windows, burning the head of Christ,
how it fell on the blood red rug and lit
the walnut pews. How I came to believe
one might be saved, not by resurrection,
but by the rapture of light playing
on the altar of song.

In the Garden

On the granite countertop in the kitchen
the vases and baskets of flowers—
lily, chrysanthemum, daisy, cyclamen,
azalea, carnation, philodendron
and a wild Christmas cactus—
brought home from the hospital
cluster like boarders
of a winter greenhouse,
the air fragrant with comfort
rather than warm cookies.
Walking by with the laundry,
I spot, out of the corner of my eye,
the purple latex garden gloves
I dropped there yesterday, before
the foliage arrived. They pose
among the blossoms and greenery,
one on top of the other, worn
by ghost hands, fingertips of the right
touched to fingertips of the left,
as though they paused
to pray, now
aware of the need.

Vigil

In the room
where we slept
I sleep
all night with my watch
in my hand,
fist swallowing the luminous
arithmetic of loss.

In my dream,
dressed in black, pencil-thin,
red scarf at your neck
you move, silent
as the second hand
stroking through aquamarine
light, my eyes tracking
you into every hour.

When morning comes
I will strap on
my watch, leather band
tight against skin
unexposed to the sun,
as though hours
were not equations
impossible

to solve, each minute
not another prayer for someone
unreturned
from the night.

Three Part Harmony

We start long before dark finding wood,
timber discarded by the waves,
downed birch, scraps from studs
and rafters. It's the last night.
No one talks of leaving,
though it joins us, the fourth
voice. The sun, as it leaves,
sparks such conflagration in the sky
the shoreline blurs with wildfire.
We're all that's left. We recall
the years of fear of nuclear war,
how we thought we would one day
scorch in the undulating cloud.

Here we offer food to flame:
hot dogs, veggie dogs,
sweet white puffs of marshmallow.
Three real dogs curl in sand
under the webbed chairs, vigilant
for the slippery wiener, the missed chip.
We don't sing, no guitars or harmonica.
But story is its own song:
a visit to the niece the dead brother
will never see; the first glimpse of ocean
for a hill child sleepy in the backseat

after an all-night drive;
a trip with the grandfather
to the dairy, grandmother churning,
the tall glass of buttermilk
mysterious and cold as the moon.

This Time in Virginia

I've come out to the gazebo to watch
the full moon rise above the staggered roofs
of the barn. Another state, another moon,
and yet another train clatters along nearby tracks.
A train can do it every time—bring up loss
like an image in developing fluid—
the clank of absence ever present in its passing.
You said last week we would soon watch
the same moon from different landscapes,
plugged into its light from separate
sockets, and so I flip the switch,
my darkness coming hours before yours,
leaving on the porch light
as I turn in to bed.

Her Granddaughter, in Church

This room smells like a hymnbook
when I put my nose inside.
But I don't need the book to sing.
I know it all by heart.

"Rock of Ages" reminds me
of the big rock, in the woods,
where sometimes we take lunch,
where Cynthia brings Winstons
she stole from her dad and Jack
is always shuffling his Bicycle
Rider Back cards, wanting to play
strip poker. Too many bugs
to take off your clothes.
My grandmother strips me
to look for ticks when I get home.
We don't want Rocky Mountain
spotted fever, she says.
No ticks at the Rock of Ages.
It's not in the Rocky Mountains.
My grandmother's best song,
the one the choir is singing now,
starts off, *I come to the garden alone.*
My grandmother's alone now,

up front in the casket,
but she's not afraid.

She'll sail it like a boat
to that beautiful shore.
She'll learn to walk on water.
She'll be waiting
to teach me.
Up yonder.

Particle or Wave

Such sadness in these early evening shadows
shed by birch trees on a county road or trail.
The seeds of grief grow if the heart lies fallow.

Shadows cast by morning sun tomorrow
will be shadows only, nothing special.
But there's sadness in these early evening shadows.

I can recall the mountain graves we mowed.
I carried water for the flowers in a pail.
The seeds of grief grow when the heart lies fallow.

Particle or wave? How can we know
the properties of light, the sliding scale
of sadness in these early evening shadows?

Out the window of my truck I watch a backhoe
scoop and chew the earth, hear its engine wail.
The seeds of grief grow where the heart lies fallow.

The light can catch you in an undertow,
a riptide of desire, a liquid tale.
Such sadness in these early evening shadows.
The seeds of grief grow if the heart lies fallow.

Elegy for Wings

On the gravel path this morning
I saw a butterfly shudder,

then realized I witnessed
a single wing, detached,

lifted by the wind, lowered
by the wind. I pinched it gently,

as though the creature who wore it once
was still attached, so thin, a slice

of silky geode. Even in dull light
it shimmered, deep blue

black, veined like a leaf, tips
of silver blue with crescent

moons, comets of orange,
and one orange sun.

Where did it voyage without its boat?
Where is its twin, the other flap

of flight? Where are such wings
that could lift my weight?

Of All the Gifts, It Was the Music

Through your headphones, which I wear
reluctantly, remembering years
of echolalia in language lab,
hymns of the Mormon Tabernacle Choir

surge through my ears like summer storm
rushing through the arroyos, rushing
unbridled in its disguise as river,
red clay banks straining to hold it in.

Despite my theology, I admit
to the grandeur of this music I can't create,
in score or voice. I don't remember
the first time you plugged me

into Scarlatti or Bach. But I do remember
a rain-slick road, front seat of a Chevy Blazer,
how the flourish of dogwood and redbud
transposed to notes in a melody I'd not heard

and never would hear again
quite the same way, though I listen
in my head and in the car as often
as I think your name.

There were other gifts, some tangible,
some not, and other rain-soaked
journeys, short and long.
Things happen.

Always there's before
and after. And now, this second
language in which sound
translates as love.

Water Aerobics, YWCA, Easter Sunday

From the hot tub where I've come to soak
my joints this Easter morning, I watch
the water aerobics class synchronize
their bodies, turning to the left, to the right,
lifting their limbs like crossing gates
when the red lights flash. Sitting in water
up to my neck, watching the class
throw up their arms like the *Glory Hallelujahs*
at those summer baptisms in Coal River,
I wonder if Jesus is here with us today,
this Sunday of Resurrection, if these bodies
wishing to give up their material selves
feel lighter, stones rolled away. Some say
there is no redemption without total
immersion, without giving in to the arms
of the river, without going under. I remember
the astonished look on the faces retrieved
from beneath the flow, open-mouthed and gasping
for air, preacher's white shirt snagged in their grasp.
There's no singing here, no praising the Lord's
name, but salvation gained in inches lost,
pounds shed. Now the litany: *Arms up,*
arms down, legs out, legs in, breathe in,
breathe out, sink low, leap up! Call

and response, sloth washed away.
We all rise up from the current,
born again.

About Darkness and Light

This morning, in moonlight, I step out
into the first snow, shovel over my shoulder,
to dig out the car at the bottom of the hill.
The snow comes to my knees, drifts
untracked in a frozen Sahara. The neighbor's
Christmas lights glow beneath white tents,
a fleet of small spaceships downed in the storm.
Everywhere around me whiteness of snow,
darkness of night. Each makes the other more
prominent. I think how I need night,
to curl safe inside its pod, how day splits
it open and rolls me out, greedy for touch.
It's like the raggle-taggle play of two cats
who share my house: the golden tabby
ferocious in his sport, the black tuxedo,
cautious and aloof, strolling to the ball.
I hear them chase through the house, catch
a glimpse of midnight eclipsing sun, see
legs and tail tangle in the hallway, flash
down the corridor like noisy comets.
They need each other though they hiss
and snarl, go searching if left alone too long.
The orange one wakes me before dawn,
a furry halo on my pillow till I rise
to fill his bowl. I stay up, unable to slip

back to sleep, flick on my Christmas lights,
put down this black ink on the blank page.
It's 4:00 A.M. and then it's 5:00, dark
outside going grey. The tree lights fade,
recede into the green caves of the limbs,
the light becoming dark, the darkness light.

Sunday Worship

for Ina Hughs

On Sunday morning driving
my truck from Taos to Santa Fe
through the rain, beside the old adobes,
shops that tempt with pottery and rugs,
moccasins and fine art, as we hum
along the Rio Grande, you say
we should sing our favorite hymns,
those songs we remember
most from all the times
we perched on varnished pews
like crows on a wire waiting
to swoop away. You start
with a hymn I've never heard
(but you're Presbyterian),
your soft voice an invocation
in this tiny chapel of steel
and glass. Because of where
we are, I follow, timid and off-key,
with "For the Beauty of the Earth,"
take my eyes from the road
to admire purple mesas,
spirits rising in the desert rain.
You take your turn, then
I take mine and soon you sing
"God of the Marching Centuries,"

tell me it was your father's favorite.
I try to recall which one
my grandmother loved the best,
and though I know it must have been
"The Old Rugged Cross," I offer up
"I Come to the Garden Alone"
preferring a less vengeful theology.
By now we have come down the mountain,
Espanola just ahead, leaving behind us
"All Things Bright and Beautiful,"
"Jacob's Ladder," and "Jesus Loves Me."
Easing into city traffic, I praise
the miracle of our lives,
how word and simple song
can resurrect the complicated past,
how years from now we both
will feel this holy morning.
As we approach the light,
you retrieve "Tell Me the Old, Old Story"
from that worn place in my heart
where the wine-robed choir sings on,
uninterrupted, where just now
I take your hand in prayer.